By Sophia Lowell

Based on the series created by Ryan Murphy & Brad Falchuk & Ian Brennan

LEVEL 2

Adapted by: Lynda Edwards

Publisher: Jacquie Bloese

Development Editor: Sarah Silver

Editor: Clare Gray

Designer: Mo Choy

Picture research: Emma Bree

Photo credits:
Cover and inside images courtesy of Twentieth Century Fox.
Page 5: Corbis/Superstock; P. Broze/Getty Images; S. Perry/iStockphoto.
Page 19: P. Broze/Getty Images.
Page 22: Photo Alto/Superstock.
Page 27: Corbis/Superstock.
Page 28: S. Perry/iStockphoto.
Page 39: P. Broze/Getty Images.
Pages 41 & 43: S. Perry/iStockphoto.
Pages 50 & 51: Blend/Superstock; Splash News, S. Amantini/Corbis;
Action Plus/Topfoto.
Pages 52 & 53: Photos India/Superstock; Cultura Creative/Alamy;
D. W. Rosier, C. Bernard/iStockphoto.

Published by Scholastic Ltd. 2012

Mary Glasgow Magazines (Scholastic Ltd.)
Euston House
24 Eversholt Street
London NW1 IDB

Printed in Singapore

Contents

	Page
Glee – Foreign Exchange	**4–47**
People and Places	**4**
High school in America	**6**
Chapter 1: News for Glee Club	**8**
Chapter 2: The French arrive	**14**
Chapter 3: Partners	**19**
Chapter 4: A surprise for Finn	**24**
Chapter 5: Clever plans	**29**
Chapter 6: Secrets and lies	**35**
Chapter 7: Party time	**38**
Chapter 8: The big performance	**42**
Chapter 9: Goodbyes and good friends	**46**
Fact Files	**48–53**
Which Glee character are you?	**48**
Basketball	**50**
Foreign exchanges	**52**
Self-Study Activities	**54–56**
New Words	**inside back cover**

TINA COHEN-CHANG is Artie's best friend.

QUINN FABRAY was the best cheerleader at McKinley High but she can't practise while she's pregnant. She really wants to be popular again.

FINN HUDSON is popular and good-looking. He's a great singer and a talented football and basketball player.

BRITTANY is a top cheerleader.

KURT HUMMEL loves fashion and stylish clothes. He prefers boys to girls and he likes Finn a lot!

SANTANA is in Glee Club and the cheerleading team.

ARTIE ABRAMS is a good singer and he's clever and funny too. He's in a wheelchair and he's not very confident with girls.

THE FRENCH STUDENTS

JEAN-PAUL is good-looking but he's very quiet and a little strange.

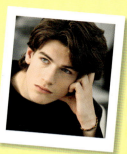

RACHEL BERRY is the star of Glee Club. She's a fantastic singer and she wants to be famous.

NOAH 'PUCK' PUCKERMAN is a football and basketball player like Finn. He thinks he's very good-looking, but he's often lazy and he's not always kind.

RIELLE sings well and also plays the guitar. She writes her own songs too.

CELESTE is the best singer in the French Glee club. She's blonde and very pretty. She's also really clever.

MERCEDES JONES is a great singer and she wears stylish clothes.

MARC is a really nice guy. Unlike the other French students, he isn't very stylish.

PLACES

MCKINLEY HIGH
The students from *Glee* all go to McKinley High School, Lima.

LIMA
All the activity in *Glee* happens in this small town in Ohio, USA. It's not an exciting town and lots of the young people can't wait to leave!

5

HIGH SCHOOL

THE STUDENTS

Students go to high school for four years, from age fourteen to eighteen years old. The people in Glee Club are in their second year at high school.

American teenagers learn a lot about themselves as well as a lot about the world at high school. They will probably meet their first boyfriend or girlfriend at high school and good friends at school can mean good friends for life!

Good **grades** (or marks) are very important too. The highest grade for homework or classwork is A; the lowest is E or F. A-grade students usually get better jobs or go to the best universities when they finish high school.

THE STAFF

High School staff are the people who work at the high school. That's not just teachers! In this Glee story, there are three important staff.

School Principal, Principal Figgins is the head of the school. He makes all the important decisions about lessons and clubs, the staff, and the school's money.

Coach, Sue Sylvester teaches McKinley High's cheerleading team. She will do anything to get more money for her cheerleaders!

Teacher, Will Schuester (or 'Mr Schu') is a McKinley High Spanish teacher – and a great performer! He plans Glee Club practices and performances.

IN AMERICA

CLUBS AND SPORTS

Clubs and sports are really important at high school. The most popular clubs and sports usually get the most money.

Here are some of the clubs and sports teams at McKinley High.

Glee Club

Glee Club is for students who are interested in performing – singing and dancing. At some high schools, Glee Clubs are very popular. But at McKinley High they are not! They often perform on a stage in the school **auditorium** for the whole school and visitors to watch.

The cheerleaders

School cheerleaders dance and do gym tricks at all the school sports games. They also 'cheer' the team – they shout the team's name in a special way. The McKinley High cheerleaders are some of the best cheerleaders in America.

The basketball team

Basketball is a popular sport in the USA and at high school. The games are an important part of high school life – students and parents go to watch.

> Read pages 48–49 to find out more about basketball – a great American game!

CHAPTER 1
News for Glee Club

It was early on a Monday morning in February and McKinley High School was empty and quiet. Kurt and his friend Mercedes arrived in Kurt's car. Kurt felt the cold wind through his thin, fashionable coat. He loved stylish clothes but they weren't always right for the weather.

'A special Glee Club meeting before school,' said Mercedes as they walked to the school door. 'Why does Mr Schu want to see us early? We've got Glee Club practice later on.' But Kurt wasn't listening. He was watching their friend Finn, the tall, good-looking football player who was getting out of his car. Finn wasn't the cleverest boy in the school but he looked great and he had a brilliant voice. Kurt smiled dreamily.

Finn walked over to them. 'Hi guys,' he said. He looked worried. 'Perhaps Mr Schu is going to leave,' he thought. The other football players thought Glee Club was for losers but Finn was different. He loved Glee Club and he didn't want it to close.

In the school corridor they met their friends Artie and Tina. Tina was pushing Artie towards the music room in his wheelchair. Artie looked clever in his thick, black glasses – and he was! But he wasn't very confident and he worried about a lot of things.

'Where's Rachel?' asked Finn. Rachel was the best singer in Glee Club. She wasn't very popular but she didn't care. She only cared about singing. She was very talented – and she knew it! When Finn stopped going out with his last girlfriend, Quinn Fabray, he and Rachel went out together a few times. They weren't together anymore but he still had special feelings for her.

In the music room, Rachel closed her eyes and sang. She always arrived half an hour early to practise singing, and she didn't hear the others come in. She finished her song and opened her eyes. 'What are you all doing here?' she asked angrily. She liked to practise alone.

'Didn't you get Mr Schu's text message?' asked Mercedes.

'No. Because I turn my phone off at night to rest my voice,' said Rachel. 'It's very important for someone with my brilliant talent.'

Mercedes stepped forward. 'We've heard enough about your brilliant talent! Why don't you …' but then Mr Schuester arrived. He was carrying a pink cake box.

'OK guys,' he said. He looked round the room. The girls from the Cheerios, the school cheerleading group, weren't there. Puck, the other footballer in Glee Club wasn't there either. 'I've got some news but a few students aren't here,' he said.

'That's OK – we can tell them later. What's the news Mr Schu?' asked Rachel.

'No, Rachel. I want to tell you all together. So let's meet again after lunch and I'll tell you then. And enjoy these.' Mr Schuester opened the box. It was full of lovely hot croissants*.

All morning the students tried to guess the news.

'I know,' smiled Rachel happily. 'Mr Schu is finally going to ask me to sing all my favourite songs from *Les Miserables***.'

'Maybe we have to sell some cakes again,' said Tina, 'so we can make more money for Glee Club.'

Then Rachel saw Quinn Fabray and her Cheerio friends

* A croissant is a kind of French breakfast bread.

** *Les Miserables* is one of the most popular shows in the world. The story and songs are about France in the early 1800s.

in the corridor. She walked over to them.

'I need to buy some clothes for the Cheerio-Basketball party,' Quinn said to her friends. She was pretty, blonde and very popular. 'Let's go shopping now.'

Rachel hated Quinn. She was pregnant but she still looked good. She was Finn's ex-girlfriend too. It wasn't fair! 'You can't go shopping,' said Rachel angrily. 'You'll miss the Glee Club meeting. Mr Schu's got some important news!'

Quinn's eyes looked mean. 'You can't stop us.'

Quinn hated Rachel too. Rachel was a loser, no one liked her. It was Rachel's fault that she and Finn weren't together. For a long time Finn thought he was the father of Quinn's baby but then Rachel told him the truth. The baby was Puck's. And now Quinn had no boyfriend.

'I can,' Rachel said confidently. 'I can tell Principal Figgins that you miss lessons all the time and go shopping!'

Then Quinn had an idea. She smiled unkindly. 'OK. We'll come to the meeting but you have to do something too. You can't talk to Finn for two weeks. OK?'

'I can't do that,' thought Rachel. But Glee Club was important. They needed the right number of people for their performances. They needed Quinn and her friends. 'OK,' she said. 'I agree.'

After lunch, all the students came to the meeting, even the Cheerios and Puck. Rachel was dreaming about a big stage. She was in the middle of it, singing a wonderful song from *Les Miserables*. Everyone was shouting, 'Rachel, Rachel!' What a moment!

Then she saw Finn. Rachel really wanted to talk to him, but then she looked at Quinn. She was smiling at Rachel. Her eyes said, 'I'm watching you!' Rachel sat down again. 'This is going to be hard!' she thought.

At last Mr Schuester came into the music room. He looked around at all the Glee Club students.

'OK. You're all here so I can tell you the news. It's about our performance for Multicultural Week.'

Every year the school had a Mulitcultural Week when they learned about other parts of the world. They had food from different countries like India and Italy in the cafeteria. At the end of the week, there was a big performance and different school groups did shows with songs and music from around the world.

Mr Schuester showed the students an old photograph of a good-looking young man. 'This is my friend Philippe,' he said. 'Philippe is French and he stayed with my family in 1994 when we were both high school students. He loved our Glee Club.'

At that time McKinley High's Glee Club was very famous and the Glee students were popular in the school.

'Philippe is a teacher now, like me, and he started a Glee Club at his school in France. He is bringing his Glee students here and we're all going to perform some songs together at the Multicultural Week show!'

This was good news! The students were excited and many started phoning friends to tell them. Puck even stopped looking at the Cheerio girls' legs. 'Wow!' he smiled. 'European girls!'

Kurt couldn't believe it. 'French students! Their clothes are so cool! Can we ask them to bring me a Louis Vuitton* bag?'

'They're arriving tomorrow! Too late Kurt,' said Mr Schuester. 'Now I want you to practise a song to perform for them when they arrive.'

Rachel's hand was up before he finished speaking. 'I can plan that!'

'I think that's a great idea,' said Quinn very sweetly. She smiled to herself. 'Rachel will be very busy,' she thought. 'She won't have time to talk to Finn!' Finn wasn't Quinn's boyfriend now, but she didn't want him to be with anyone else. Certainly not Rachel!

* Louis Vuitton is the name of a French fashion business.

Chapter 2
The French arrive

The last lesson on Monday was Mr Thorne's English class. Artie loved English and always got As for his homework. Puck was in the same class and slept all the time – with his eyes open!

'Here's your homework,' said Mr Thorne as he gave them a new book. 'It's a play called *Cyrano de Bergerac** and it's a love story. Cyrano has a problem. Women don't like him because he has a very big nose!'

Artie was interested. Perhaps he could learn something from Cyrano. He had a problem too – not a big nose, but a big wheelchair.

'I want three pages about Cyrano before Friday,' Mr Thorne said.

'I haven't done English homework for two years!' laughed Puck. He smiled confidently at Mr Thorne and some of the girls in the class laughed.

Artie didn't understand girls. Why did they all like

* *Cyrano de Bergerac* is a famous French play written in 1897 by Edmond Rostand.

Puck? He wasn't clever and he was often unkind to people like Artie. Once he locked Artie in a cupboard for a few hours. Just for fun! Perhaps it was because Puck was a big, strong footballer and Artie was thin and wore glasses. Life was hard. 'It was probably hard for Cyrano too,' thought Artie.

In the music room after school Rachel was excited. She had plans for the Glee Club performance.

'We'll sing *Lady Marmalade*,*' she explained. 'It's a fantastic song and parts of it are in French! Also we've got some great little black dresses and red dance shoes to wear. Very French!'

'So, you went shopping in school time?' Quinn smiled. 'Who's missing lessons now?'

'I got the clothes from French Club,' said Rachel coldly.

'That's really great, Rachel!' smiled Finn.

Rachel wanted to kiss him but she couldn't even speak to him. 'Two weeks without speaking to Finn!' she thought. 'Why did I agree?'

'Good song Rachel,' said Mr Schuester. 'Let's practise!'

Rachel tried hard to think about the song and not Finn. Quinn watched her and smiled to herself. This was fun!

It was Tuesday lunchtime and the students were in the cafeteria. It was Mexican food because it was Multicultural Week and everyone ate a lot. It smelled wonderful and Rachel wanted to try some, but she decided to eat her apple instead. She never ate a lot before an important performance.

* *Lady Marmalade* is a hit song from the 1970s by American girl group, LaBelle.

15

'Do you think the French will be good singers?' asked Mercedes.

'I hope not,' thought Rachel. She always wanted to be the best. 'I hope the girls aren't pretty either,' she thought too.

Puck had different ideas. 'French girls are cool,' he smiled. 'And they will all want me!' he said confidently. 'I'm going to be busy!'

'I hope they all look like stars from a French black and white film – beautiful, stylish, different,' said Kurt, dreamily.

Mr Schuester came into the cafeteria. He found the Glee students and walked up to their table. 'OK,' he smiled, 'Let's go and meet the French students!'

The Glee Club students went to the auditorium to get ready for the performance but something felt wrong.

'It's very hot in here,' said Quinn. It was snowing outside now. She wanted to run outside and jump in it!

'I don't feel very well,' Tina's head hurt too.

'My mouth is very dry,' said Santana. 'And I can still smell my lunch.'

'Are you OK Rachel?' Finn asked but Rachel turned away. 'What's the matter with her? Have I done something wrong?' he thought.

Everyone got dressed in their stylish French clothes. 'I can't wait to perform,' thought Rachel. 'Where are the French students?'

Suddenly, the door opened and a tall man came in with a group of students. Mr Schuester was very excited! He kissed the French teacher, Philippe, twice in the French way.

'I like that idea,' thought Kurt. He thought about getting close to Finn like that every day.

Philippe was very good-looking and his voice was soft. The Cheerio girls were suddenly more interested in the French visitors than before.

'Wow!' said Santana. 'I'm in love! I mean – I know he's a teacher but he's French. That's OK, isn't it?'

'Welcome to McKinley High Glee Club!' Mr Schuester said to the French group. 'The students would like to perform for you. I hope you enjoy it!'

All the Glee Club students went on the stage and they started their song. Rachel was enjoying it but there was something wrong with Mercedes' voice. It wasn't as strong as it usually was. Then suddenly Santana ran off the stage. What was happening?

'Oh no,' shouted Quinn and she ran off too. Tina followed her. One by one all the students left the stage until only Rachel was singing. She liked singing alone but this wasn't the right time!

The French students looked at their teacher. This was a very unusual performance! First the students sang a song with very strange French words in it and then they all ran off the stage! Was this an American joke?

'I'm very sorry about this!' said Mr Schuester and he went outside to see what was wrong.

When he came back his face was red. 'The students are all ill!' he said. 'I think they have food poisoning from today's lunch!'

'This is a terrible start for the Glee Club!' thought Rachel, smiling quickly at Philippe and the French students. Suddenly she was very pleased that she only had her apple at lunchtime!

Chapter 3
Partners

On Wednesday morning the Glee Club students were feeling much better. It was time for them to meet the French students. Mr Schuester gave all the Glee Club students a French partner. He wanted the American students to show the French students around the school. Also, he wanted them to be friends.

Rachel was having problems with her partner. He was a tall, thin boy with long, dark hair called Jean-Paul. He looked unhappy and bored.

He didn't smile and he didn't speak. Rachel had lots of ideas for things to do but he preferred listening to his music and talking on his mobile phone! He only looked interested once – when he saw Finn and his French partner Celeste. 'Who's that?' he asked.

'That's Finn,' explained Rachel. She liked talking about Finn. She knew everything about him. 'He's a footballer and he plays basketball too. He's a real star.' But now

Rachel was unhappy too. Celeste was blonde and very beautiful with a lovely smile. She and Finn were having a long conversation and their faces were nearly touching!

Quinn also saw them. It wasn't fair. Quinn's partner, Nicholas, was very quiet and wore glasses like Artie. 'Why does Finn get Celeste?' she thought. 'And why do I get this loser?' Then she had an idea. She pulled her partner along the corridor and went up to Finn. She gave him and Celeste a big smile.

'Finn,' she said brightly. 'Let's go round school together. You and Celeste and me and … him.'

'OK,' said Finn. He was feeling very pleased. Celeste was the best partner. She was pretty and clever and she spoke four languages! Her English was very good and she seemed to like him. She was a bit like Quinn, but cleverer and nicer!

Mr Schuester took Philippe to meet Principal Figgins. The Principal worked very hard and he was often very tired. McKinley High was a big school and there were always problems. He felt very tired today, as usual, but he had a smile for Philippe.

'It's good to meet you!' said Figgins. 'I like France. You have lots of beautiful women there!' Then he stopped smiling and listened. He heard a sound he knew very well. Sue Sylvester's feet in the corridor. He walked slowly towards the door. Sue was always trouble.

The tall, blonde Cheerios coach came into the office. She was angry.

'Who are the strange non-American people in our school?' she asked, looking first at Figgins, then at Mr Schuester. Her voice was like a knife. Nothing about Sue was sweet or soft.

'Sue! Sue!' said Figgins quickly. 'They are our French friends. They're with Will's Glee Club students for Multicultural Week.'

'Ah!' Sue looked at Mr Schuester like she was looking at some dirt on her trainers. 'Glee Club! Those losers. I understand now.'

Principal Figgins started speaking again. 'I have some news about the Multicultural Week performances. Mr Doherty is going to be at the show. If he likes it there may be some more money for our clubs!' Mr Doherty was an important man in Lima. He decided about money for the schools in the area.

Sue's Cheerios club already had a lot of money but Sue was always looking for more. 'OK,' she decided quickly. 'My Cheerios will perform too.'

Mr Schuester looked at Sue angrily. 'Your Cheerios can't do a performance in Multicultural Week! They're a sports group!'

'Oh no?' Sue was taller than Mr Schuester and she looked down on the top of his head. She almost felt sorry for him. Almost, but not completely. 'My Cheerios can do anything. And they can do it better than your losers! See you at the show!' and she walked out confidently.

Philippe didn't understand. Who was this crazy woman? A teacher? They didn't have teachers like her in France. America was a very strange country.

Puck was having a bad day too. His partner, Gerard, was more interested in American food than Puck's questions about French girls. He was even more interested in Puck's basketball friends than Puck himself! Puck couldn't understand it.

'It isn't fair,' he thought. 'Finn gets the beautiful Celeste and Artie's got the pretty Rielle! Those girls need a real American man – not those boys.'

Then his day got worse. Puck saw Kurt. He was waving at a group of French girls. The girls were talking and laughing. One of them, Aimee, was smiling and flirting with Kurt.

'Kurt! You are really stylish!' Aimee called out.

Then Aimee's friends joined in. 'Kurt. I love your clothes.'

'Kurt. You are just like a French boy. I love your shoes and your hair!'

Kurt laughed. He loved all this talk about fashion. These girls thought he looked great! He didn't know that they were flirting with him. They didn't only like his clothes!

'Well, they've got that wrong,' thought Puck. 'Kurt prefers boys! Everyone can see that. This is so unfair.'

Then he saw Rielle in the corridor. 'OK. It's my time now,' he smiled. He put his back against the wall and looked lazily at Rielle. 'I look really cool,' he thought. But Rielle walked past him. What? This was bad! Nobody walked past Puck without a look. What was he doing wrong?

Chapter 4
A surprise for Finn

For the first time in their lives the Glee Club students were popular. Everyone wanted to meet and talk to the French students. They were talented, clever, interesting and they wore great clothes.

Well, they all wore great clothes except Mercedes' partner, Marc. Mercedes really liked Marc but his clothes were terrible. He didn't know anything about style. Luckily Mercedes did. She loved fashion and she looked cool. 'I can help him,' she thought. 'He's a really nice guy.'

'Let's go shopping later,' she said when they were in the cafeteria.

'OK,' said Marc but he wasn't really listening. He was looking at the strange meatballs on his plate. 'Do you eat this every day?'

'Usually it's worse!' joked Mercedes. After the food poisoning yesterday the cafeteria decided to cook something easy. They called it 'Italian' but it wasn't very good.

Then Mr Schuester came in with Philippe. The teachers waved at Mercedes and Marc and smiled. The Cheerio girls were at another table in the cafeteria and they were alone. Mr Schuester walked over to them.

'Where are your French students?' he asked.

Santana didn't look up from her magazine. It wasn't cool to talk to teachers. 'Oh – we gave them to Kurt,' she said.

Mr Schuester couldn't believe it, but it was true! Kurt had French girls all round him. They were talking about fashion again. Kurt's eyes were shining. He pointed to a girl in a magazine. 'Versace is fine but not as good as Jean Paul Gaultier's* new spring look.'

'Girls don't usually flirt with Kurt!' thought Mr Schuester. 'But it's good to see them all so happy.'

In the winter the footballers at McKinley High usually did basketball instead and they practised in the gymnasium. Today the Cheerios were practising there too with Coach Sylvester.

Quinn watched them from her seat. Once she was the best Cheerio but now Santana was Coach Sylvester's favourite. Quinn didn't like being pregnant. She preferred being popular.

* Versace and Jean Paul Gaultier are top European fashion businesses.

Rachel and her strange French partner were watching the basketball.

'There he is,' she pointed to Finn. Jean-Paul didn't like anything Rachel did. She showed him different places in the school and told him all about her life at McKinley High but he wasn't interested. So she brought him to basketball practice. He seemed to like Finn.

'Perhaps he likes sport and thinks girls are boring,' she thought.

'Who is the best player?' asked Jean-Paul.

'Finn, he's fantastic,' said Rachel. Her heart always jumped when she saw Finn playing basketball. He was stronger and taller than the other players and very quick. But today her heart felt heavy. Finn was with Celeste. He was showing her some moves with the basketball and Celeste was clearly flirting with him. They were laughing and touching.

Quinn saw it too. 'This is bad,' she thought. 'Celeste is a bigger problem than Rachel. Rachel is a loser, but Celeste is different. She's dangerous.'

Suddenly Jean-Paul stood up. 'I want to go now,' he said. He looked angry.

Rachel followed him out of the gymnasium. She felt terrible. Maybe Multicultural Week wasn't such a good idea.

Artie and his partner Rielle arrived at the music room early for practice. Artie was fine with that. It gave him a little more time alone with her. He liked Rielle a lot. She was pretty but she was also really cool. She carried her guitar everywhere and she wrote her own songs. Artie watched and listened to Rielle as she played one of her own songs.

But Artie had a problem. It was hard for him to talk about his feelings because he wasn't very confident. His wheelchair was like a wall between him and the girl he liked.

'Can you write some words for my music?' asked Rielle.

Artie's face went pink. 'Oh yes!' he said, 'I'd love to.' Perhaps this was the answer. His words could tell her about his feelings. Like Cyrano did in the play!

After basketball practice Finn was the last student in the showers. He and Celeste talked for a long time after practice, and now he was late for Glee Club. But he was very happy and he sang loudly in the shower. When he finished he put a towel around him.

'What's that lovely smell?' he thought. Then he turned and saw Celeste. Why was Celeste here in the boys' shower room? Finn closed his eyes but when he opened them again she was still there. She was sitting still and watching Finn carefully. She looked very, very pretty!

'How did you get in here?' asked Finn.

'There is a … door?' Celeste laughed sweetly. She smiled slowly at Finn. 'I like your towel,' she said softly.

Finn's face was red. 'But-'

Celeste moved quickly and kissed him. Her hands were in his hair.

'This is nice,' thought Finn. 'Very nice!'

Finn moved back and looked at Celeste. His heart was going fast. 'I am so happy that you like me. I wasn't sure. I like you too, Celeste. I like you very much!'

Suddenly Celeste's eyes changed. The light was gone and she was looking at Finn very strangely.

'It's late. We must go to Glee practice. Hurry up,' she said quietly. She turned away and left the room.

'What happened?' thought Finn. But his heart felt light as he got dressed. It was a very, very good day!

Chapter 5
Clever plans

All the Glee Club students were in the music room except Finn. Puck was sitting alone, playing the drums. He wanted people to look at his strong arms – especially Rielle. But Rielle wasn't looking at him. She was laughing and singing with Artie and the others. 'They're all losers,' Puck thought. 'Can't she understand that?' Even his partner Gerard didn't need him. He was practising some dance moves with another basketball player.

Rachel was sitting alone too. Jean-Paul didn't want to talk to her. What was his problem? Didn't he understand that she was brilliant and talented?

When Finn arrived he had a stupid smile on his face. He looked around the music room quickly and then sat down next to Celeste. Quinn and Rachel looked at him. Why was he smiling like that?

'Hi!' he said to Celeste. But she didn't smile back at him. Finn looked hurt and Quinn and Rachel both felt much happier.

Celeste jumped up without looking at Finn and joined her French friends at the front of the room. The French Glee Club was ready to perform their song.

It was a brilliant performance. The song was fast and difficult but all the French Glee students were great singers. It was clear that Celeste was their star.

Rachel felt cold. 'It isn't fair,' she thought. 'Celeste is beautiful, popular *and* she has a fantastic voice.'

'She's wonderful!' smiled Mercedes, to Kurt and Tina. 'I thought my voice was big but hers is even stronger!'

'She dances really well too,' smiled Tina. 'She's really talented.'

'She's like a young Vanessa Paradis,' said Kurt to Tina. 'That's Johnny Depp's French ex-girlfriend,' he explained.

'Celeste sang in a French show when she was younger,' said Finn. As usual Rachel was listening. 'What!' she nearly shouted. 'Which show?'

'*Les Miser*… somethings,' Finn said.

Rachel nearly fell off her chair. Her favourite show! This French girl had everything that she wanted. Probably Finn too!

'That was fantastic!' said Mr Schuester when the French students finished. Everyone was clapping loudly and Mr Schuester's face was shining. 'Thank you all!' he smiled. 'Now, for our performance together we're going to put a French song and an American song together,' he explained.

'Sing in French? I've only just learned good English!' Puck laughed and looked at Rielle but she was smiling at Artie.

'You can learn the words with your French partners,' said Mr Schuester.

Then Rachel had an idea. A very good one.

When Mr Schuester saw Rachel come towards him his head started to hurt. This often happened when Rachel talked to him.

'Mr Schu,' she said brightly. 'I've got an idea. I'd like Celeste to be my partner. We're both the stars of our groups and she could learn a lot from me.'

Mr Schuester looked at her.

Rachel corrected herself. 'I mean – I can learn a lot from her too. We can both learn.'

Before he could say anything, Rachel continued. 'And Jean-Paul likes Finn – so they'll be good together!'

'OK, Rachel,' agreed Mr Schuester. 'I'm sure Jean-Paul will be happier with Finn than Rachel,' he thought. 'His head probably hurts when he's around Rachel too!'

Her plan was going to be a success! Rachel ran over to Celeste and Finn to tell them about the change. Finn was talking to Celeste.

'Would you like to come with me to the Cheerio-Basketball party?' he asked her. Rachel's heart dropped. Oh no! This was worse than she thought. But Celeste didn't answer Finn.

'Hi Rachel,' she said instead, 'You were fantastic yesterday. You've got a lovely voice!'

Rachel smiled. 'Thank you! I've got some good news. Mr Schu says that we can be partners now!' Finn wasn't happy but Celeste seemed very pleased.

Rachel turned to Finn. 'Jean-Paul thinks you're great,' she told him. 'He wants to hear all about your basketball.'

'Oh yes,' thought Rachel. 'This is a good plan.'

Artie and Rielle were together in the corridor after class. Their heads were close and they were laughing. Puck wasn't happy. 'I need to do something,' he thought. 'That girl is too good for Artie.' He walked over to them slowly. Puck never did anything quickly.

'Artie! My friend!' he smiled.

'Oh no,' thought Artie. 'What does he want?'

'I need your help. This *Cyrano de* … something. I need to get an A in my homework or Principal Figgins will stop my basketball. And my Glee.' He tried to look worried. 'You always have great ideas. Can I use some for my homework?'

Rielle was smiling at Puck. 'Is she flirting with him?' thought Artie.

'OK,' said Artie. 'You can have my book after school.' He looked at Rielle. 'Now she knows I'm a nice guy,' he thought.

'Sweet!' Puck gave Artie a big smile. Then he turned to Rielle. 'It's cool that you play the guitar. And I hear you write music. Maybe I can write some words for you.'

Artie nearly died! Puck – write songs? But Rielle went red. 'Thank you. I'd like that,' she said.

'Cool.' Puck gave Rielle one of his special deep looks and then walked away lazily.

Rielle laughed. 'He is such a … bad boy?' Then she touched Artie's arm. 'Do you want to go shopping later?'

Artie's heart felt a lot lighter. 'I'm sorry Rielle – I'm going to be busy.'

'Yes,' he thought. 'Very busy. I need to write a very good song!'

Mercedes took Marc to Lima's shopping centre. She chose a fashionable shop and found some new jeans and a shirt for Marc. She waited outside the room while he put them on. It was very busy. A lot of McKinley High students were there. Santana and Brittany from the Cheerios came into the shop.

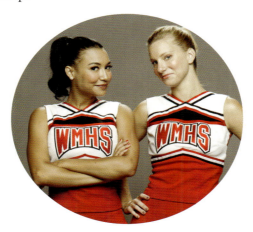

'What are you doing here? This is a shop for fashionable people!' said Santana. 'And where's your strange French partner? His clothes are really bad!'

'Forget about the French students,' said Brittany. 'Forget about Glee Club. We have to practise our Cheerios performance for the show.'

'Yes,' agreed Santana. 'And we need to get some cool clothes for the party. You know – the party the Glee Club can't come to!' They laughed and walked off.

Mercedes' face was hot. 'I hope Marc didn't hear them,' she thought. But when he came out of the room he was very angry.

'Those girls think they are film stars!' he said. 'We must go to that party. We can invite ourselves!'

Mercedes smiled. 'Yes,' she said. 'Glee Club can have some fun too. I can't wait to see Santana's face!'

Chapter 6
Secrets and lies

The cafeteria was busy and very noisy so Rachel and
Celeste took their lunch to the gymnasium. Finn was
practising basketball inside. Rachel's heart lifted when he
waved. But then she saw that he was waving at Celeste.

Celeste looked at Rachel. 'Is Finn like all American
boys?' she asked.

Rachel thought. Yes, Finn liked sports and games and
music – the same as other American boys. But he was
different too. He joined Glee Club. He didn't care that
people thought Glee Club students were losers.

'Not really,' she replied. 'What are French boys like?'

Celeste smiled. 'That's a hard question. French boys are
… difficult. They don't want to talk about their feelings.'

'American boys too. Sometimes they stop liking you
and you don't know why.' Rachel felt sad.

Celeste looked at her carefully. Then she looked at Finn.
Her blue eyes shone. 'No!' she said. 'You and Finn … you
were girlfriend and boyfriend?'

Rachel's face went red. She didn't want to talk to
Celeste about Finn.

'I don't understand. Why are you sad? Finn is a nice
guy … but he isn't a great guy!'

Rachel couldn't believe it. 'What? You don't like him?'

'He's OK. I wanted to try … you know, with an
American boy, but he's a bit strange. He just looks at me
all the time.' Celeste tried her Indian meal. It was quite
good.

Suddenly Rachel's day was much, much better.

'Anyway,' Celeste continued. 'I have decided to forget

about boys. My last boyfriend really hurt me. Now I want to think about my singing and my future.'

'I completely agree with you!' Rachel said brightly.

Celeste's blue eyes shone happily. 'You know, I really like you Rachel. We're the same. It's good that we are partners.'

Rachel looked quickly at Finn. Her heart still jumped when she saw him but Celeste was right. Music was more important than boys.

Rachel walked along the corridor after her last class. She felt good. 'Celeste is pretty, but she doesn't like Finn!' she smiled. 'And she's going back to France soon. Yes!'

Then she saw Quinn and Santana. They were going home. Suddenly Rachel got angry.

'Where are you going?' she asked. 'You missed practice this morning. We need you!'

Quinn looked at Rachel coldly. 'We're leaving Glee Club. It's your fault. You spoke to Finn. I said two weeks. It was only four days!' Quinn put on her expensive coat carefully. It didn't fit well now because she was pregnant but she still looked like a film star. She smiled and waved as she and Santana went outside into the cold. 'Goodbye, loser!' she said.

Rachel's face went white. 'OK,' she thought. 'They want a fight? I can give them one!' Rachel turned and walked quickly down the corridor. There was something that Principal Figgins needed to know!

The Cheerios were missing from Glee Club practice again. Mr Schuester found them in the gymnasium. They were practising with Sue Sylvester for the Cheerios'

performance. They were working hard. It was very, very hot in the room because Sue thought it made her girls stronger.

'Faster,' she shouted. 'Faster!'

'Santana, Brittany!' Mr Schuester called to his Cheerios. 'Are you coming to Glee Club practice?'

Sue smiled. She knew the girls couldn't leave now. Not in front of their friends.

'We can't,' said Santana. She felt a bit sorry for Mr Schuester. But the Cheerios were more important.

'OK,' said Mr Schuester. 'We'll miss you. Come back if you want to.'

'They won't be back,' Sue smiled confidently. 'They're Cheerios, not losers.'

Artie was worried. He couldn't find the songs he wrote for Rielle. Then he remembered. They were in the book he gave to Puck. When Puck gave it back Artie turned the pages quickly.

'Where are my songs?' he nearly shouted.

'Oh, I gave them to Rielle,' said Puck with a smile. 'I wanted her to think I am clever. You know – like Cyrano. He used another guy's words to make a girl love him.' Puck felt a bit bad – but not very bad. 'It's cool! She loved them. She's coming to the party with me too. Thanks Artie!'

Chapter 7
Party time

Quinn was very tired. She slept in the library and when she woke up it was dark outside. She went outside into the car park.

She had a problem. Everyone was talking about Finn and Celeste and she felt sad. She was pregnant and getting bigger and bigger. Her old boyfriend was following a beautiful French girl round like a little dog! She needed a partner for tomorrow's party and she wanted her confidence back. Then she saw Puck by his car and she had an idea.

'Hi Puck!' she smiled. 'Did you miss me at Glee Club?'

Puck looked surprised. 'You weren't there? I was thinking about something else.'

Quinn wasn't pleased. That wasn't the right answer. She moved closer. 'Are you going to the party Puck?' she asked in her sweetest voice. 'I bought a new dress.'

Puck laughed. 'Oh yes! I've got plans. And her name is Rielle! Sorry Quinn. Maybe I'll choose you another time!' He jumped into his car and drove away.

Quinn's face went red. 'No!' She thought. 'Nobody chooses me second!' She looked quickly around the car park, hoping no one saw Puck drive away.

Jean-Paul, the quiet French guy, was sitting outside in the cold. Quinn thought quickly. 'The American boys won't like seeing me at the party with a French boy!' she smiled as she walked towards Jean-Paul.

'Hi,' she said. 'There's a party tomorrow night. You're coming with me. OK?'

Jean-Paul didn't say anything at first. He didn't even look up.

'Will Finn be there?' he asked, at last.

'Why is everyone interested in Finn at the moment?' Quinn thought. 'He'll be there,' she said.

Jean-Paul looked up at her. 'OK. I will come,' he said.

'Good', said Quinn. Now she had a plan too. And his name was Jean-Paul!

The music at the party was very loud. The big house was full of students and lights shone from every window. It was very hot inside.

There were a lot of girls at the party but Finn thought he had the prettiest partner. Celeste was beautiful in her blue top and black jeans. But she was very quiet and when Finn put his hand on her arm she moved away.

'What's wrong with her?' thought Finn. He didn't know what to say to Celeste. With Rachel that was never a problem! But Rachel didn't talk to him now. Girls! He couldn't understand them.

On the sofa, Puck was sitting close to Rielle. Their legs were nearly touching. Rielle was still surprised by Puck's wonderful songs. They were really clever and funny. There were even some French words in the songs. But now, at the party, Puck wasn't saying very much.

Quinn wasn't having a good time at the party either. What was Jean-Paul's problem? She watched him as he followed Finn and Celeste across the room. Then some students got up to dance.

'OK,' she thought. 'Everyone's looking now. It's time for me to do something!'

Quinn followed Jean-Paul and stood in front of him. 'Do you want to dance?' she asked softly, her mouth close against his ear. Before he could answer, Quinn kissed him. Everyone pointed and shouted! But Jean-Paul's face went white and he pulled away.

Behind him Celeste ran out of the room and into the garden. Jean-Paul followed her.

Quinn didn't understand. Jean-Paul didn't want to kiss her? Was that possible?

'Did you see that?' she asked Santana. 'That crazy French guy kissed me. I couldn't stop him!'

Things got worse for Quinn. A group of students arrived at the party. Quinn couldn't believe it. It was the Glee Club students and their French partners. And they all looked good – even the French boy that always dressed badly!

'Hey! It's SingStar!'* Kurt took the group into a room where some students were singing with a video game. He and Mercedes sang a song from the 1960s. Everyone started singing and dancing and clapping. At last the party was fun!

Outside, the night was clear and cold. Finn watched Jean-Paul and Celeste in the garden. They were talking loudly in French and then Jean-Paul took Celeste's arm.

* SingStar is a music video game where people can sing to music.

'Stop that!' shouted Finn. He ran into the garden.

'No Finn,' Celeste went in front of Jean-Paul. 'It's OK. Jean-Paul was once my boyfriend. I didn't like it when he kissed Quinn. He just came to see that I was OK.'

'Your ex-boyfriend? Do you still … have feelings for him?' asked Finn.

Celeste looked at Finn. 'It's difficult. When you stop going out with someone, your feelings don't just stop.'

She felt sorry for Finn. He looked so sad. 'I'm sorry Finn. I was having fun. That's all.'

Finn got angry. 'Well – you're crazy – both of you!' He ran back inside the house. Then he thought about Celeste's words. 'Your feelings don't just stop.' Some of the Glee students were at the party. Was Rachel here too? His heart started to go a little faster. Perhaps girls weren't the only crazy ones.

Chapter 8
The big performance

It was Saturday night and time for the Multicultural Show. Behind the stage everyone was excited. In the auditorium a lot of people were waiting for the performances. Mr Doherty and his wife were at the front.

Principal Figgins went to say 'Good luck' to the students. First he saw some Chinese dancers and then an Irish group. Next to them were the Cheerios. They were holding pictures of people from different countries.

'Coach Sylvester!' called Principal Figgins, pointing at Santana and Brittany. 'I told you yesterday. Those girls can't perform. Rachel tells me they've missed too many lessons and their teachers agree. They need to learn!'

Principal Figgins looked angry, but Sue wasn't really listening. 'Figgins,' she said. 'That's crazy. I need them in the group.' She looked at all the people in the auditorium. They were waiting to watch *her* girls.

'No Sue. I'm sorry, but I have decided. Girls!' he called. 'Either you don't perform or you perform with Glee Club. Those French students can teach you a lot of things!'

Sue's face went white. This was terrible for her group. 'I won't forget this,' she said. 'This is a big mistake, Principal Figgins.'

Mr Schuester was very pleased to see the two Cheerios join Glee Club for the performance. There was only one problem.

'Has anyone seen Celeste?' he asked. The Irish group was finishing and the Cheerios were ready to go on stage. It was Glee Club's turn very soon!

'I'll find her,' shouted Rachel and she ran down the corridor. Celeste was sitting on the stairs. She looked sad. Rachel sat beside her.

'Are you OK Celeste?' she asked. 'It's our turn soon.'

Celeste's eyes were red. 'It's Jean-Paul,' she said. 'I don't want to see him. He's my ex-boyfriend – the one who hurt me. Now he wants to go out with me again. I don't know what to do!'

'I'm not the best person to help with a love problem,' thought Rachel. But she wanted Celeste to be happy. 'You mustn't be sad because of a boy!' she said. 'You're more important than he is!'

'I don't want to see him. I can't perform with him!'

'Celeste,' Rachel said carefully. 'Think about your Glee Club. They need you. You're their best singer!'

Celeste was quiet for a moment. Then she lifted her head. 'You're right Rachel,' she said strongly. 'I *am* their best singer. They can't continue without me. I don't care about Jean-Paul!' Then she stood up. 'Let's go. Our stage is waiting!'

Mr Schuester was starting to get worried. The Cheerios' performance was nearly over. Where were Rachel and Celeste?

Suddenly the two girls appeared. 'Quickly,' said Mr Schuester. 'It's time!'

The Glee Club students walked out onto a dark stage with the French students. It was very quiet. Then the lights were on, the drums started and the students began singing and dancing. It was a brilliant performance and everybody loved them. Rachel closed her eyes. She loved the sound of the shouting and clapping. It was wonderful!

Mr Schuester was clapping too. It was the best performance of the night. 'Mr Doherty will love this!' he thought. 'More money for the Glee Club will be great!' He watched the American and French students singing together. 'Those students have done something wonderful together this week. That's the real success!'

Chapter 9
Goodbyes and good friends

The French students were leaving on Sunday morning and everyone in Glee Club went to say goodbye. Even the Cheerios were there.

It was a bright, cold, sunny day but everyone was sad. The American and French students were now good friends.

'We didn't get more money for Glee Club,' Mr Schuester told Philippe. 'Because of the food poisoning they decided the cafeteria needed new fridges!'

Philippe laughed. 'I think that's a good idea! Goodbye Will. We had a great time.'

Celeste gave Rachel her address. 'Tell me when you're a star,' she said. 'And thank you for everything.'

Artie couldn't get close to the bus in his wheelchair. Rielle came over to him and gave him a kiss.

'Merci* Artie,' she said softly, 'the songs are beautiful!'

Artie was surprised. 'You knew it wasn't Puck?'

Rielle smiled. 'Of course! I knew at the party. He is … not very clever! And he can't speak French!' she laughed. 'Please send me some more!'

Kurt's French girls were the last on the bus. They kissed him and started to cry. 'Write to us Kurt! We love you!'

'I will miss you all,' called Kurt as the bus drove off. Everyone was waving.

Puck turned to Kurt. 'How did you do that?'

* 'Merci' means 'thank you' in French.

he asked. 'The girls love you. The other guys – and me – we couldn't get a French girlfriend!' He thought for a moment. 'And you don't like girls anyway!' He just couldn't understand.

'Ah!' said Kurt with a smile. 'That's my secret!'

WHICH glee™

CHARACTER ARE YOU?

We all have a Glee character inside us. Do this quiz to find yours!

 1 What time do you get to school?

a   15 minutes late. Who cares?

b   Always on time. Always looking good.

c   5 minutes late so everyone can see me arrive.

d   30 minutes early, to practise my singing.

e   When I finish my exercises.

2 You see a new girl walking in the corridor; you:

a   Show them how strong you are.

b   Show them your new Marc Jacobs jacket.

c   Wait until *they* come to *you*.

d   Smile, and then talk about yourself.

e   Talk to them when other people aren't around.

3 ⭐ **What's your favourite drink?**

a Anything cold (it's just to throw at someone).

b Water. It's good for my skin.

c Diet Coke. That's what all the girls drink.

d Warm milk, for my throat, of course.

e A sports drink, like coach told me.

4 ⭐ **Lunchtime! Where do you sit?**

a With the jocks, of course.

b Lunchtime is for shopping, not eating!

c At the table with all the popular students.

d Who has time for lunch? I want to practise my singing!

e I don't mind – I just want lots to eat!

5 ⭐ **What will you wear for your school photo?**

a Something cool to show my strong arms.

b My new Armani shirt!

c My cheerleading clothes! What else?

d Something to help me look like a star.

e Something comfortable and sporty.

Which Glee character do you like most? Why?

ANSWERS

How many a,b,c,d and e answers did you get? Count them and then choose the right Glee character.

Mostly a

You're most like Puck. You love being cool and you love the girls! But be careful: nice girls don't like bullies!

Mostly b

You're most like Kurt. Looking good is everything to you. Remember: your friends have feelings. Clothes aren't everything!

Mostly c

You're most like Quinn. Being popular is very important to you. Be careful that you don't finish your school life with no real friends at all.

Mostly d

You're most like Rachel. You know what you want and you're ready to work hard to get it. Don't forget to listen to other people too!

Mostly e

You're most like Finn. You're a nice person, but you don't really know what you want. Don't try to do too much!

What do these words mean? You can use a dictionary.

character   skin   throat   jock   bully

49

BASKETBALL

Finn and Puck are footballers but they play a lot of basketball too. Everything about basketball in the US is very AMERICAN and very BIG!

IT'S AMERICAN!

Basketball started in America in 1891. A teacher in Massachusetts called Dr James Naismith wanted to invent an indoor game for his football students to play in bad winter weather. Women started to play the next year and soon it was popular all over the USA and Canada. But it wasn't famous internationally until the Olympic Games in 1992.

The rules have changed a lot since 1891. But you still need a basket, five people on each team and a ball. The idea is to get the ball through your opposing team's basket. Children in the street or at school can play basketball easily because you don't need much equipment – a bit like football!

Like the American Dream, basketball makes people believe that the impossible is possible!

IT'S BIG!

Big people: In a real game the basket (or the 'hoop') must be 10 feet above the floor … If you're tall it helps! One of the tallest basketball players in the world is Paul 'Tiny' Sturgess (2.318m tall). In this photo he is standing next to his team mate, Jonte 'Too Tall' Hall (1.57m tall).

Big crowds: Today, millions of people watch basketball in the USA. The teams are as popular as football teams in Europe!

Big money: The best players in top teams can get a lot of money – up to $25 million a year!

THE DREAM TEAM

In 1992 the USA basketball team won the Olympics with a fantastic team. It was called the Dream Team.

Some people say that the 1992 Dream Team was the best team there has ever been in any sport in the world. The players were like film stars or rock stars and everyone wanted to see them.

Even today, many people have heard the names Michael Jordan, Larry Bird and 'Magic' Johnson. They inspired today's superstar players, such as LeBron James and Kobe Bryant.

Which sports do you like to play or watch?

What do these words mean? You can use a dictionary.

invent   rule   equipment   tiny   rock star   inspire

FOREIGN EXCHANGES

Philippe and his French students came to McKinley High on a foreign exchange. Here, we find out more about foreign exchanges.

WHAT ARE THEY?

People visit other countries to learn more about other cultures and people. They exchange ideas, learn new languages and make new friends.

WHO ORGANISES THEM?

Many foreign exchanges are organised by schools and universities. Some people organise their own exchanges with friends in other countries. There are also special organisations that can organise the exchanges for you. For example, the AFS helps students to find exchange places in more than 50 countries.

HOW CAN I GO?

First talk to your parents and teachers or look on the Internet for exchange organisations. You need to plan when you can go and where you can stay. You may also need to work or save money before you go.

REAL LIFE EXCHANGES

Name: Elsie Lennox
Age: 16
From: Birmingham, England
Visited: The Durant family, Bordeaux, France

I stayed with a French family for ten days. They were very kind – and they owned their own vineyard, which was really cool! I ate a lot of different food and I loved it. My French got a lot better and I made some very good friends. It was brilliant.

Name: Ikumi Tanaka
Age: 17
From: Yokohama, Japan
Visited: The Markes family, Queensland, Australia

I stayed with a family in Queensland for six months. Their life was very different to mine in Japan. They lived on a farm but I live in a city. Also, people need cars for everything in Australia – but I can't drive! I enjoyed my time but six months is very long and I got a bit homesick. When I came home, I looked at my life differently.

Name: Colin Mannion
Age: 17
From: Chicago, USA
Visited: The Santorini family, Milan, Italy

I spent a year in Italy and it was the best year of my life! I learned a lot about the culture but more than that I learned about myself. I became independent and you need to be away from your family and home to do that. Also I made some wonderful friends who I hope I will have for the rest of my life.

Would you like to go on an exchange? Where?

What do these words mean? You can use a dictionary.

culture   organisation   vineyard   homesick   independent

CHAPTERS 1–2

Before you read

1 Choose the right words. You can use a dictionary.
   a) Singers and dancers usually perform on a *stage / corridor*.
   b) You must cook meat well, or you may get *food poisoning / performance*.
   c) The young mother *missed / kissed* her baby on his head.
   d) Let's eat dinner in the *cafeteria / auditorium* before we watch the *staff / show*.

2 Match the sentences.
   a) She can sing very well.   i)   She's pregnant.
   b) Her clothes are fashionable.   ii) It's multicultural.
   c) She's going to have a baby.   iii) She's confident.
   d) She knows she's pretty and popular.   iv) She's talented.
   e) The show has songs from many countries.   v)   They're stylish.

3 Read 'People and Places' and 'High School in America' on pages 4–7. Do you think the American students and the French students will become good friends? Why / why not?

After you read

4 Answer the questions.
   a) Why do the students have to go to school early?
   b) What is Mr Schuester's news?
   c) Why is Artie interested in Cyrano de Bergerac?
   d) Why can't Rachel talk to Finn?
   e) What do many of the students eat for lunch?
   f) Which song do the Glee Club students sing for the French students? Why?

5 What do you think? How do Philippe and his students feel after their first day in America?

CHAPTERS 3–5

Before you read

6 Complete the sentences with the correct words. You can use a dictionary.

clap   crazy   heart   gymnasium   drums   flirt   towel

   a) The students practise basketball in the … .
   b) The … were very loud during the performance!
   c) An old … is best for the beach.
   d) My … felt heavy when I heard the sad news.
   e) At the end of the show, everyone stood up and … .
   f) Maria is …! She does very strange things.
   g) 'Don't … with Katy. She's my girlfriend!'

7 Will Rachel talk to Finn in these chapters? Give reasons for your answer.

After you read

8 Are these sentences true or false? Correct the false sentences.
   a) Finn likes his partner very much.
   b) Principal Figgins enjoys talking to Sue.
   c) The Cheerios are going to perform at the show.
   d) The French girls think Puck is good-looking.
   e) The students have Mexican food again in the cafeteria.
   f) Both the Cheerios and the basketball team are in the gymnasium.
   g) Puck wants Rielle to help him with his homework.

9 Match the questions and answers.
   a) Who is the star of the French Glee Club?   **i)** Jean Paul Gaultier
   b) What's the name of a famous French show?   **ii)** to the Cheerio-Basketball party
   c) Where does Mercedes go with Marc?   **iii)** Celeste
   d) Who is a famous fashion designer?   **iv)** Les Miserables
   e) Where can't Glee Club students go?   **v)** to the shopping centre

10 What do you think? What do these people feel about each other?
- **a)** Celeste and Rachel
- **b)** Jean-Paul and Finn
- **c)** Puck and Rielle

CHAPTERS 6–9

Before you read

11 What do you think? What will happen …
- **a)** at the party?
- **b)** at the performance?
- **c)** at the end of the story?

After you read

12 Put these parts of the story in order.
- **a)** Rachel finds Celeste on the stairs.
- **b)** Mr Schuester goes to the Cheerios' practice.
- **c)** Quinn kisses Jean-Paul at the party.
- **d)** Rachel and Celeste watch basketball and talk about boys.
- **e)** The Glee Club students and the French do a brilliant performance.
- **f)** Quinn and Santana leave Glee Club.
- **g)** Rielle kisses Artie.
- **h)** Quinn talks to Puck and Jean-Paul in the car park.
- **i)** Artie gets his notebook from Puck.

13 What do you think?
- **a)** Will the American students miss the French students? Why / why not?
- **b)** Did the American and French students learn anything from each other? What did they learn?